The Hagopian Institute, LLC has compiled the Quote Junkie series. The overall series includes over 8,000 quotes, focusing mostly on short quotes that can be used in everyday life as sources of wisdom and inspiration. This is a special edition focusing solely on quotes that are ten words or less. These quotes are perfect for managers, coaches, inspirational speakers, or just the average Joe who enjoys spewing wisdom when out with their friends. These quotes all have well-known authors, and are simple and easy to remember. You will enjoy searching for those perfect words to end a presentation, a pep talk, or a consultation. Please enjoy, and share these quotes with your co-workers, friends and family.

Todd Hagopian

President

The Hagopian Institute, LLC

Great necessities call out great virtues.

Abigail Adams

A house divided against itself cannot stand.

Abraham Lincoln

Everybody likes a compliment.

Abraham Lincoln

I can make more generals, but horses cost money.

Abraham Lincoln

I walk slowly, but I never walk backward.

Abraham Lincoln

I will prepare and some day my chance will come.

Abraham Lincoln

If I were two-faced, would I be wearing this one?

Abraham Lincoln

Public opinion in this country is everything.

Abraham Lincoln

The ballot is stronger than the bullet.

Abraham Lincoln

What kills a skunk is the publicity it gives itself.

Abraham Lincoln

Whatever you are, be a good one.

Abraham Lincoln

A war for a great principle ennobles a nation.

Albert Pike

Faith begins where Reason sinks exhausted.

Albert Pike

War is a series of catastrophes which result in victory.

Albert Pike

Will is the dynamic soul-force.

Albert Pike

Instinct is untaught ability.

Alexander Bain

A promise must never be broken.

Alexander Hamilton

I have learned to hold popular opinion of no value.

Alexander Hamilton

I think the first duty of society is justice.

Alexander Hamilton

Man is a reasoning rather than a reasonable animal.

Alexander Hamilton

Those who stand for nothing fall for anything.

Alexander Hamilton

I am dying from the treatment of too many physicians.

Alexander The Great

There is nothing impossible to him who will try.

Alexander The Great

Liars need to have good memories.

Algernon Sydney

It is always the simple that produces the marvelous.

Amelia Barr

Old age is the verdict of life.

Amelia Barr

The inevitable has always found me ready and hopeful.

Amelia Barr

There is little success where there is little laughter.

Andrew Carnegie

Disunion by force is treason.

Andrew Jackson

One man with courage makes a majority

Andrew Jackson

The Bible is the rock on which this Republic rests.

Andrew Jackson

To the victors belong the spoils.

Andrew Jackson

War is a blessing compared with national degradation.

Andrew Jackson

I am a mystery to myself.

Angelina Grimke

We Abolition Women are turning the world upside down.

Angelina Grimke

Nothing is miserable unless you think it is so.

Anicius Manlius Severinus Boethius

There is always a "but" in this imperfect world.

Anne Bronte

Issue the orders Sir, and I will storm Hell.

Anthony Wayne

Observe your enemies, for they first find out your faults.

Antisthenes

A friend to all is a friend to none.

Aristotle

All men by nature desire knowledge.

Aristotle

All paid jobs absorb and degrade the mind.

Aristotle

Bad men are full of repentance.

Aristotle

Change in all things is sweet.

Aristotle

Education is the best provision for old age.

Aristotle

Fear is pain arising from the anticipation of evil.

Aristotle

Friendship is a single soul dwelling in two bodies.

Aristotle

Good habits formed at youth make all the difference.

Aristotle

Happiness depends upon ourselves.

Aristotle

Man is by nature a political animal.

Aristotle

Most people would rather give than get affection.

Aristotle

No excellent soul is exempt from a mixture of madness.

Aristotle

No one loves the man whom he fears.

Aristotle

Philosophy is the science which considers truth.

Aristotle

Pleasure in the job puts perfection in the work.

Aristotle

Quality is not an act, it is a habit.

Aristotle

The law is reason, free from passion.

Aristotle

The secret to humor is surprise.

Aristotle

The whole is more than the sum of its parts.

Aristotle

The young are permanently in a state resembling intoxication.

Aristotle

Those that know, do. Those that understand, teach.

Aristotle

We make war that we may live in peace.

Aristotle

Well begun is half done.

Aristotle

Wit is educated insolence.

Aristotle

Every happiness is a hostage to fortune.

Arthur Helps

Man's action is only a picture book of his creed.

Arthur Helps

Will minus intellect constitutes vulgarity.

Arthur Schopenhauer

The only thing I am afraid of is fear.

Arthur Wellesley

Hasten slowly.

Augustus

A beautiful woman should break her mirror early.

Baltasar Gracian

A single lie destroys a whole reputation of integrity.

Baltasar Gracian

Aspire rather to be a hero than merely appear one.

Baltasar Gracian

Be content to act, and leave the talking to others.

Baltasar Gracian

Friendship multiplies the good of life and divides the evil.

Baltasar Gracian

Know or listen to those who know.

Baltasar Gracian

Let the first impulse pass, wait for the second.

Baltasar Gracian

Never contend with a man who has nothing to lose.

Baltasar Gracian

Never have a companion that casts you in the shade.

Baltasar Gracian

Quit while you're ahead. All the best gamblers do.

Baltasar Gracian

Respect yourself if you would have others respect you.

Baltasar Gracian

The things we remember best are those better forgotten.

Baltasar Gracian

True knowledge lies in knowing how to live.

Baltasar Gracian

Without courage, wisdom bears no fruit.

Baltasar Gracian

Work is the price which is paid for reputation.

Baltasar Gracian

Laws undertake to punish only overt acts.

Baron de Montesquieu

Liberty is the right to do what the law permits.

Baron de Montesquieu

Peace is a natural effect of trade.

Baron de Montesquieu

The less men think, the more they talk.

Baron de Montesquieu

Useless laws weaken the necessary laws.

Baron de Montesquieu

All things excellent are as difficult as they are rare.

Baruch Spinoza

Happiness is a virtue, not its reward.

Baruch Spinoza

Will and intellect are one and the same thing

Baruch Spinoza

Change is inevitable. Change is constant.

Benjamin Disraeli

Desperation is sometimes as powerful an inspirer as genius.

Benjamin Disraeli

Diligence is the mother of good fortune.

Benjamin Disraeli

Ignorance never settles a question.

Benjamin Disraeli

Little things affect little minds.

Benjamin Disraeli

Man is only great when he acts from passion.

Benjamin Disraeli

The fool wonders, the wise man asks.

Benjamin Disraeli

The secret of success is constancy to purpose

Benjamin Disraeli

There is no education like adversity.

Benjamin Disraeli

A man wrapped up in himself makes a very small bundle.

Benjamin Franklin

A penny saved is a penny earned.

Benjamin Franklin

All wars are follies, very expensive and very mischievous ones.

Benjamin Franklin

Be slow in choosing a friend, slower in changing.

Benjamin Franklin

By failing to prepare, you are preparing to fail.

Benjamin Franklin

Fatigue is the best pillow.

Benjamin Franklin

Guests, like fish, begin to smell after three days.

Benjamin Franklin

Half a truth is often a great lie.

Benjamin Franklin

He that rises late must trot all day.

Benjamin Franklin

He that speaks much, is much mistaken.

Benjamin Franklin

Honesty is the best policy.

Benjamin Franklin

In this world nothing is certain but death and taxes.

Benjamin Franklin

Keep your eyes wide open before marriage, half shut afterwards.

Benjamin Franklin

Many foxes grow gray but few grow good.

Benjamin Franklin

Necessity never made a good bargain.

Benjamin Franklin

Never confuse motion with action.

Benjamin Franklin

Observe all men, thyself most.

Benjamin Franklin

One today is worth two tomorrows.

Benjamin Franklin

Some people die at 25 and aren't buried until 75.

Benjamin Franklin

Take time for all things: great haste makes great waste.

Benjamin Franklin

The doors of wisdom are never shut.

Benjamin Franklin

The strictest law sometimes becomes the severest injustice.

Benjamin Franklin

The worst wheel of the cart makes the most noise.

Benjamin Franklin

There was never a good war, or a bad peace.

Benjamin Franklin

Those that won't be counseled can't be helped.

Benjamin Franklin

Three can keep a secret, if two of them are dead.

Benjamin Franklin

Time is money.

Benjamin Franklin

To lengthen thy life, lessen thy meals.

Benjamin Franklin

Whatever is begun in anger ends in shame.

Benjamin Franklin

When in doubt, don't.

Benjamin Franklin

When you're finished changing, you're finished.

Benjamin Franklin

Who is rich? He that rejoices in his portion.

Benjamin Franklin

Wise men don't need advice. Fools won't take it.

Benjamin Franklin

You may delay, but time will not.

Benjamin Franklin

Absence sharpens love, presence strengthens it.

Benjamin Franklin

An investment in knowledge always pays the best interest.

Benjamin Franklin

Drive thy business or it will drive thee.

Benjamin Franklin

Employ thy time well, if thou meanest to get leisure.

Benjamin Franklin

Energy and persistence conquer all things.

Benjamin Franklin

He that can have patience can have what he will.

Benjamin Franklin

He that cannot obey, cannot command.

Benjamin Franklin

He that lives upon hope will die fasting.

Benjamin Franklin

If passion drives you, let reason hold the reins.

Benjamin Franklin

Lost time is never found again.

Benjamin Franklin

Well done is better than well said.

Benjamin Franklin

Wish not so much to live long as to live well.

Benjamin Franklin

Great lives never go out; they go on.

Benjamin Harrison

The bud of victory is always in the truth.

Benjamin Harrison

Passion is the drunkenness of the mind.

Bishop Robert Smith

Wonder is from surprise, and surprise stops with experience.

Bishop Robert Smith

Eloquence is a painting of the thoughts.

Blaise Pascal

Kind words do not cost much. Yet they accomplish much.

Blaise Pascal

Law, without force, is impotent.

Blaise Pascal

Man's greatness lies in his power of thought.

Blaise Pascal

Noble deeds that are concealed are most esteemed.

Blaise Pascal

Our nature consists in motion; complete rest is death.

Blaise Pascal

The heart has its reasons of which reason knows nothing.

Blaise Pascal

Two things control men's nature, instinct and experience.

Blaise Pascal

We only consult the ear because the heart is wanting.

Blaise Pascal

You always admire what you really don't understand.

Blaise Pascal

The way to have power is to take it.

Boss Tweed

Honest hearts produce honest actions.

Brigham Young

Love the giver more than the gift.

Brigham Young

A jug fills drop by drop.

Buddha

Ambition is like love, impatient both of delays and rivals.

Buddha

He is able who thinks he is able.

Buddha

It is better to travel well than to arrive.

Buddha

Peace comes from within. Do not seek it without.

Buddha

The foot feels the foot when it feels the ground.

Buddha

The mind is everything. What you think you become.

Buddha

Those who are free of resentful thoughts surely find peace.

Buddha

It takes a great man to be a good listener.

Calvin Coolidge

Knowledge comes, but wisdom lingers.

Calvin Coolidge

No man ever listened himself out of a job.

Calvin Coolidge

I praise loudly. I blame softly.

Catherine The Great

In life, as in chess, forethought wins.

Charles Buxton

Power ought to serve as a check to power.

Charles de Secondat

A boy's story is the best that is ever told.

Charles Dickens

A loving heart is the truest wisdom.

Charles Dickens

He would make a lovely corpse.

Charles Dickens

Let us be moral. Let us contemplate existence.

Charles Dickens

Regrets are the natural property of grey hairs.

Charles Dickens

'Tis love that makes the world go round, my baby.

Charles Dickens

Vices are sometimes only virtues carried to excess!

Charles Dickens

We forge the chains we wear in life.

Charles Dickens

You don't carry in your countenance a letter of recommendation.

Charles Dickens

Freedom is a system based on courage.

Charles Peguy

Tyranny is always better organized than freedom.

Charles Peguy

Judicious absence is a weapon.

Charles Reade

Make 'em laugh; make 'em cry; make 'em wait.

Charles Reade

A ruffled mind makes a restless pillow.

Charlotte Bronte

Better to be without logic than without feeling.

Charlotte Bronte

Conventionality is not morality.

Charlotte Bronte

Give him enough rope and he will hang himself.

Charlotte Bronte

I feel monotony and death to be almost the same.

Charlotte Bronte

Let your performance do the thinking.

Charlotte Bronte

Look twice before you leap.

Charlotte Bronte

Good words will not give me back my children.

Chief Joseph

I am tired of talk that comes to nothing.

Chief Joseph

I will speak with a straight tongue

Chief Joseph

It does not require many words to speak the truth.

Chief Joseph

Mediocre men often have the most acquired knowledge.

Claude Bernard

Acquaintance lessens fame.

Claudius

No one is free who does not lord over himself.

Claudius

And remember, no matter where you go, there you are.

Confucius

Better a diamond with a flaw than a pebble without.

Confucius

Everything has its beauty but not everyone sees it.

Confucius

Forget injuries, never forget kindnesses.

Confucius

He who will not economize will have to agonize.

Confucius

Never give a sword to a man who can't dance.

Confucius

Only the wisest and stupidest of men never change.

Confucius

Real knowledge is to know the extent of one's ignorance.

Confucius

The cautious seldom err.

Confucius

To go beyond is as wrong as to fall short.

Confucius

We should feel sorrow, but not sink under its oppression.

Confucius

When anger rises, think of the consequences.

Confucius

Wherever you go, go with all your heart.

Confucius

You cannot open a book without learning something.

Confucius

Our opportunities to do good are our talents

Cotton Mather

Poverty breeds lack of self-reliance.

Daniel de Leon

A wise man proportions his belief to the evidence.

David Hume

And what is the greatest number? Number one.

David Hume

Beauty in things exists in the mind which contemplates them.

David Hume

Custom is the great guide to human life.

David Hume

Everything in the world is purchased by labor.

David Hume

Men often act knowingly against their interest.

David Hume

The law always limits every power it gives.

David Hume

Truth springs from argument amongst friends.

David Hume

The world ultimately is what we say it is.

David Strauss

Business is other people's money.

Delphine de Girardin

Instinct is the nose of the mind.

Delphine de Girardin

The best religion is the most tolerant.

Delphine de Girardin

By desiring little, a poor man makes himself rich.

Democritus

Hope of ill gain is the beginning of loss.

Democritus

Men should strive to think much and know little.

Democritus

The wrongdoer is more unfortunate than the man wronged.

Democritus

Concealed talent brings no reputation.

Desiderius Erasmus

Don't give your advice before you are called upon.

Desiderius Erasmus

Fools are without number.

Desiderius Erasmus

He who allows oppression shares the crime.

Desiderius Erasmus

Humility is truth.

Desiderius Erasmus

Prevention is better than cure.

Desiderius Erasmus

The desire to write grows with writing.

Desiderius Erasmus

Time takes away the grief of men.

Desiderius Erasmus

War is sweet to those who have not experienced it.

Desiderius Erasmus

Women, can't live with them, can't live without them.

Desiderius Erasmus

Your library is your paradise.

Desiderius Erasmus

Blushing is the color of virtue.

Diogenes of Sinope

I know nothing, except the fact of my ignorance.

Diogenes of Sinope

It takes a wise man to discover a wise man.

Diogenes of Sinope

Most men are within a finger's breadth of being mad.

Diogenes of Sinope

The mob is the mother of tyrants.

Diogenes of Sinope

Why not whip the teacher when the pupil misbehaves?

Diogenes of Sinope

Disaffection stalks around us.

Dolley Madison

Time is the fairest and toughest judge.

Edgar Quinet

What we share with another ceases to be our own.

Edgar Quinet

I fight fairly, and in good faith.

Edmund About

The blessings we evoke for another descend upon ourselves.

Edmund Gibson

One threatens the innocent who spares the guilty

Edward Coke

Success in crime always invites to worse deeds.

Edward Coke

Things are worth what they will fetch at a sale

Edward Coke

Where there are many counsellors there is safety.

Edward Coke

Corruption, the most infallible symptom of constitutional liberty.

Edward Gibbon

Our work is the presentation of our capabilities.

Edward Gibbon

I hate getting bored.

Edward Hall

An ounce of loyalty is worth a pound of cleverness.

Elbert Hubbard

Live truth instead of professing it.

Elbert Hubbard

Positive anything is better than negative nothing.

Elbert Hubbard

The love we give away is the only love we keep.

Elbert Hubbard

There is no failure except in no longer trying.

Elbert Hubbard

To avoid criticism, do nothing, say nothing, and be nothing.

Elbert Hubbard

We work to become, not to acquire.

Elbert Hubbard

A woman's always younger than a man of equal years.

Elizabeth Barrett Browning

Every wish is like a prayer -with God.

Elizabeth Barrett Browning

God's gifts put man's best dreams to shame.

Elizabeth Barrett Browning

I work with patience, which is almost power.

Elizabeth Barrett Browning

If you desire faith, then you have faith enough.

Elizabeth Barrett Browning

Light tomorrow with today!

Elizabeth Barrett Browning

My sun sets to raise again.

Elizabeth Barrett Browning

Two human loves make one divine.

Elizabeth Barrett Browning

A little credulity helps one on through life very smoothly.

Elizabeth Gaskell

I will make you shorter by the head.

Elizabeth I

The past cannot be cured.

Elizabeth I

The stone often recoils on the head of the thrower.

Elizabeth I

Honest people don't hide their deeds.

Emily Bronte

Terror made me cruel.

Emily Bronte

All philosophy lies in two words, sustain and abstain.

Epictetus

Control thy passions lest they take vengence on thee.

Epictetus

Difficulties are things that show a person what they are.

Epictetus

Do not laugh much or often or unrestrainedly.

Epictetus

Freedom is the right to live as we wish.

Epictetus

If you wish to be a writer, write.

Epictetus

No great thing is created suddenly.

Epictetus

Communism is in conflict with human nature.

Ernest Renan

Idleness is to the human mind like rust to iron.

Ezra Cornell

Affairs that depend on many rarely succeed.

Francesco Guicciardini

A prudent question is one-half of wisdom.

Francis Bacon

Anger makes dull men witty, but it keeps them poor.

Francis Bacon

For also knowledge itself is power.

Francis Bacon

God hangs the greatest weights upon the smallest wires.

Francis Bacon

It is impossible to love and to be wise.

Francis Bacon

Opportunity makes a thief.

Francis Bacon

Rebellions of the belly are the worst.

Francis Bacon

The worst men often give the best advice.

Francis Bacon

The worst solitude is to have no real friendships.

Francis Bacon

He who defends everything defends nothing.

Frederick II

As savage as a bear with a sore head.

Frederick Marryat

Every moment of resistance to temptation is a victory.

Frederick William Faber

Every moment of resistance to temptation is a victory.

Frederick William Faber

All truth is simple... is that not doubly a lie?

Friedrich Nietzsche

Faith: not wanting to know what is true.

Friedrich Nietzsche

He who laughs best today, will also laughs last.

Friedrich Nietzsche

Idleness is the parent of psychology.

Friedrich Nietzsche

In heaven, all the interesting people are missing.

Friedrich Nietzsche

That which does not kill us makes us stronger.

Friedrich Nietzsche

The best weapon against an enemy is another enemy.

Friedrich Nietzsche

The doer alone learneth.

Friedrich Nietzsche

The lie is a condition of life.

Friedrich Nietzsche

There are no facts, only interpretations.

Friedrich Nietzsche

Wit is the epitaph of an emotion.

Friedrich Nietzsche

Woman was God's second mistake.

Friedrich Nietzsche

If there is no God, everything is permitted.

Fyodor Dostoevsky

Realists do not fear the results of their study.

Fyodor Dostoevsky

The greatest happiness is to know the source of unhappiness.

Fyodor Dostoevsky

The soul is healed by being with children

Fyodor Dostoevsky

To live without Hope is to Cease to live.

Fyodor Dostoevsky

Education is the art of making man ethical.

Georg Wilhelm Friedrich Hegel

I'm not ugly, but my beauty is a total creation.

Georg Wilhelm Friedrich Hegel

Avarice is the vice of declining years.

George Bancroft

By common consent gray hairs are a crown of glory

George Bancroft

The public is wiser than the wisest critic.

George Bancroft

Flippancy, the most hopeless form of intellectual vice.

George Gissing

Have the courage of your desire.

George Gissing

The only cure for grief is action.

George Henry Lewes

A traitor is everyone who does not agree with me.

George III

Marriage is a mistake every man should make.

George Jessel

Attitudes are more important than facts.

George Macdonald

Love is the opener as well as closer of eyes.

George Macdonald

The principle part of faith is patience.

George Macdonald

Always imitate the behavior of the winners when you lose.

George Meredith

Caricature is rough truth.

George Meredith

Don't just count your years, make your years count.

George Meredith

Kissing don't last: cookery do!

George Meredith

Memoirs are the backstairs of history.

George Meredith

She poured a little social sewage into his ears.

George Meredith

The well of true wit is truth itself.

George Meredith

Education: A debt due from present to future generations.

George Peabody

Admiration and familiarity are strangers.

George Sand

Few men have virtue to withstand the highest bidder.

George Washington

Guard against the impostures of pretended patriotism.

George Washington

Happiness and moral duty are inseparably connected.

George Washington

If we are wise, let us prepare for the worst.

George Washington

It is better to offer no excuse than a bad one.

George Washington

The Constitution is the guide which I never will abandon.

George Washington

To err is natural; to rectify error is glory.

George Washington

Worry is the interest paid by those who borrow trouble.

George Washington

Time takes all and gives all.

Giordano Bruno

With luck on your side, you can do without brains

Giordano Bruno

Good council has no price.

Giuseppe Mazzini

Above all nations is humanity.

Goldwin Smith

Personality is lower than partiality.

Goldwin Smith

I have tried so hard to do right.

Grover Cleveland

Officeholders are the agents of the people, not their masters.

Grover Cleveland

Some day I will be better remembered.

Grover Cleveland

I hate artists who are not of their time.

Guillaume Apollinaire

Joy always came after pain.

Guillaume Apollinaire

One can't carry one's father's corpse about everywhere.

Guillaume Apollinaire

A friend who dies, it's something of you who dies.

Gustave Flaubert

Anything becomes interesting if you look at it long enough.

Gustave Flaubert

Everything which one invents is true, be sure of it.

Gustave Flaubert

Exuberance is better than taste.

Gustave Flaubert

Happiness is a monstrosity! Punished are those who seek it.

Gustave Flaubert

Reality does not conform to the ideal, but confirms it.

Gustave Flaubert

Success is a consequence and must not be a goal.

Gustave Flaubert

The future is the worst thing about the present.

Gustave Flaubert

The heart, like the stomach, wants a varied diet.

Gustave Flaubert

The more humanity advances, the more it is degraded.

Gustave Flaubert

There is no truth. There is only perception.

Gustave Flaubert

What an elder sees sitting; the young can't see standing.

Gustave Flaubert

What is the beautiful, if not the impossible.

Gustave Flaubert

Every great dream begins with a dreamer.

Harriet Tubman

You'll be free or die!

Harriet Tubman

Addresses are given to us to conceal our whereabouts.

Hector Hugh Munro

Great Socialist statesmen aren't made, they're still-born.

Hector Hugh Munro

I always say beauty is only sin deep.

Hector Hugh Munro

Clever people will recognize and tolerate nothing but cleverness.

Henri Frederic Amiel

Common sense is calculation applied to life.

Henri Frederic Amiel

Order is power.

Henri Frederic Amiel

The best path through life is the highway.

Henri Frederic Amiel

To marry unequally is to suffer equally.

Henri Frederic Amiel

All experience is an arch, to build upon.

Henry B. Adams

Friends are born, not made.

Henry B. Adams

Morality is a private and costly luxury.

Henry B. Adams

Philosophy: Unintelligible answers to insoluble problems.

Henry B. Adams

Politics are a very unsatisfactory game.

Henry B. Adams

Practical politics consists in ignoring facts.

Henry B. Adams

Susceptibility to the highest forces is the highest genius.

Henry B. Adams

The proper study of mankind is woman.

Henry B. Adams

Be not simply good; be good for something.

Henry David Thoreau

Be true to your work, your word, and your friend.

Henry David Thoreau

Dreams are the touchstones of our character.

Henry David Thoreau

Goodness is the only investment that never fails.

Henry David Thoreau

it is never too late to give up your prejudices

Henry David Thoreau

Men are born to succeed, not fail.

Henry David Thoreau

The language of friendship is not words but meanings.

Henry David Thoreau

Things do not change; we change.

Henry David Thoreau

Conscience - the only incorruptible thing about us.

Henry Fielding

Guilt has very quick ears to an accusation.

Henry Fielding

It is not death, but dying, which is terrible.

Henry Fielding

Love and scandal are the best sweeteners of tea

Henry Fielding

One fool at least in every married couple.

Henry Fielding

What's vice today may be virtue, tomorrow.

Henry Fielding

Where the law ends tyranny begins.

Henry Fielding

How many men are there who fairly earn a million dollars?

Henry George

To do a common thing uncommonly well brings success.

Henry J Heinz

Don't let your studies interfere with your education.

Henry Rutgers

On an exhausted field, only weeds grow.

Henry Sienkiewicz

A thought often makes us hotter than a fire.

Henry Wadsworth Longfellow

All things come round to him who will but wait.

Henry Wadsworth Longfellow

Into each life some rain must fall.

Henry Wadsworth Longfellow

Love gives itself; it is not bought.

Henry Wadsworth Longfellow

Every charitable act is a stepping stone toward heaven.

Henry Ward Beecher

Gratitude is the fairest blossom which springs from the soul.

Henry Ward Beecher

Our best successes often come after our greatest disappointments.

Henry Ward Beecher

A man's character is his fate.

Heraclitus

Big results require big ambitions.

Heraclitus

Bigotry is the sacred disease.

Heraclitus

Deliberate violence is more to be quenched than a fire.

Heraclitus

Much learning does not teach understanding.

Heraclitus

Nothing endures but change.

Heraclitus

The eyes are more exact witnesses than the ears.

Heraclitus

The sun is new each day.

Heraclitus

A jury is composed of twelve men of average ignorance.

Herbert Spencer

All socialism involves slavery.

Herbert Spencer

How often misused words generate misleading thoughts.

Herbert Spencer

Marriage: A word which should be pronounced "mirage".

Herbert Spencer

Our lives are universally shortened by our ignorance.

Herbert Spencer

A smile is the chosen vehicle of all ambiguities.

Herman Melville

Art is the objectification of feeling.

Herman Melville

To be called one thing, is oftentimes to be another.

Herman Melville

Truth is in things, and not in words.

Herman Melville

All men's gains are the fruit of venturing.

Herodotus

Circumstances rule men and not men circumstances.

Herodotus

Death is a delightful hiding place for weary men.

Herodotus

Great deeds are usually wrought at great risks.

Herodotus

Illness strikes men when they are exposed to change.

Herodotus

In soft regions are born soft men.

Herodotus

Men trust their ears less than their eyes.

Herodotus

Of all possessions a friend is the most precious.

Herodotus

The destiny of man is in his own soul.

Herodotus

A flow of words is a sure sign of duplicity.

Honore de Balzac

A man is a poor creature compared to a woman.

Honore de Balzac

A mother who is really a mother is never free.

Honore de Balzac

Behind every great fortune lies a great crime.

Honore de Balzac

Bureaucracy is a giant mechanism operated by pygmies.

Honore de Balzac

Clouds symbolize the veils that shroud God.

Honore de Balzac

Finance, like time, devours its own children.

Honore de Balzac

Love is a game in which one always cheats.

Honore de Balzac

Love is the poetry of the senses.

Honore de Balzac

Manners are the hypocrisy of a nation.

Honore de Balzac

Men die in despair, while spirits die in ecstasy.

Honore de Balzac

Modesty is the conscience of the body.

Honore de Balzac

The more one judges, the less one loves.

Honore de Balzac

Those who spend too fast never grow rich.

Honore de Balzac

When law becomes despotic, morals are relaxed, and vice versa.

Honore de Balzac

A mugwump is a person educated beyond his intellect.

Horace Porter

Be moderate in everything, including moderation.

Horace Porter

Desperate affairs require desperate measures.

Horatio Nelson

Repression will provoke rebellion.

Hugh Williamson

I will burn your city, your land, your self.

Hulagu Khan

I will toss you in the air like a lion.

Hulagu Khan

Science is organized knowledge. Wisdom is organized life.

Immanuel Kant

To be is to do.

Immanuel Kant

Acquaint yourself with your own ignorance.

Isaac Watts

Learning to trust is one of life's most difficult tasks.

Isaac Watts

Women... can't live with 'em... can't shoot 'em.

Ivan Turgenev

Affluence means influence.

Jack London

A person possessed with an idea cannot be reasoned with.

James Anthony Froude

Fear is the parent of cruelty.

James Anthony Froude

Human improvement is from within outward.

James Anthony Froude

The essence of greatness is neglect of the self.

James Anthony Froude

I like the noise of democracy.

James Buchanan

The tendency of democracies is, in all things, to mediocrity.

James F. Cooper

A law is not a law without coercion behind it.

James Garfield

A pound of pluck is worth a ton of luck.

James Garfield

Ideas control the world.

James Garfield

Justice and goodwill will outlast passion.

James Garfield

Nobody but radicals have ever accomplished anything in a great crisis.

James Garfield

Right reason is stronger than force.

James Garfield

Suicide is not a remedy.

James Garfield

Why do men fight who were born to be brothers?

James Longstreet

If men were angels, no government would be necessary.

James Madison

Philosophy is common sense with big words.

James Madison

A little flattery will support a man through great fatigue.

James Monroe

National honor is the national property of the highest value.

James Monroe

A man is accountable to no person for his doings.

James Otis

A man's house is his castle.

James Otis

Taxation without representation is tyranny.

James Otis

Kids will reach whatever expectation you set for them.

James Sullivan

Nobility, without virtue, is a fine setting without a gem.

Jane Porter

Out of difficulties grow miracles.

Jean de la Bruyere

Age doesn't matter, unless your cheese.

Jean Paul

Be great in act, as you have been in thought.

Jean Paul

A feeble body weakens the mind.

Jean-Jacques Rousseau

Patience is bitter, but its fruit is sweet.

Jean-Jacques Rousseau

All we ask is to be let alone.

Jefferson Davis

Every law is an infraction of liberty.

Jeremy Bentham

Tyranny and anarchy are never far apart.

Jeremy Bentham

Intuition is the clear conception of the whole at once.

Johann Kaspar Lavater

The public seldom forgive twice.

Johann Kaspar Lavater

A government of laws, and not of men.

John Adams

Fear is the foundation of most governments.

John Adams

Great is the guilt of an unnecessary war.

John Adams

Liberty cannot be preserved without general knowledge among the people.

John Adams

Property is surely a right of mankind as real as liberty

John Adams

The happiness of society is the end of government.

John Adams

The result showed the wisdom of your orders.

John Bigelow

Force is not a remedy.

John Bright

Popular applause veers with the wind.

John Bright

To survive, men and business and corporations must serve.

John Henry Patterson

Those who own the country ought to govern it.

John Jay

Government has no other end, but the preservation of property.

John Locke

No man's knowledge here can go beyond his experience.

John Locke

What worries you, masters you.

John Locke

The humblest is the peer of the most powerful.

John Marshall Harlan

I have not yet begun to fight!

John Paul Jones

Evil prospers when good men do nothing.

John Philpot Curran

His smile is like the silver plate on a coffin.

John Philpot Curran

Where annual elections end is where slavery begins.

John Quincy Adams

All good things which exist are the fruits of originality.

John Stuart Mill

I can never consent to being dictated to.

John Tyler

Nothing comes merely by thinking about it.

John Wanamaker

I believe that in the end truth will conquer.

John Wycliffe

Books, the children of the brain.

Jonathan Swift

No wise man ever wished to be younger.

Jonathan Swift

Promises and pie-crust are made to be broken.

Jonathan Swift

There is nothing in this world constant but inconstancy.

Jonathan Swift

A grain of poetry suffices to season a century.

Jose Marti

A selfish man is a thief.

Jose Marti

Charm is a product of the unexpected.

Jose Marti

It is necessary to make virtue fashionable.

Jose Marti

Mountains culminate in peaks, and nations in men.

Jose Marti

Learn to think impartially.

Joseph Chamberlain

You cannot teach old dogs new tricks.

Joseph Chamberlain

Every country has the government it deserves.

Joseph De Maistre

Flattery is like cologne water, to be smelt, not swallowed.

Josh Billings

It ain't often that a man's reputation outlasts his money.

Josh Billings

He who knows how to be poor knows everything.

Jules Michelet

You are one of the forces of nature.

Jules Michelet

I never could be good when I was not happy

Julia Ward Howe

Marriage, like death, is a debt we owe to nature.

Julia Ward Howe

Cowards die many times before their actual deaths.

Julius Caesar

Experience is the teacher of all things.

Julius Caesar

I came, I saw, I conquered.

Julius Caesar

Democracy is the road to socialism.

Karl Marx

History repeats itself, first as tragedy, second as farce.

Karl Marx

I am not a Marxist.

Karl Marx

Religion is the opium of the masses.

Karl Marx

Revolutions are the locomotives of history.

Karl Marx

The only antidote to mental suffering is physical pain.

Karl Marx

To secure peace is to prepare for war.

Karl Von Clausewitz

Politics is the womb in which war develops.

Karl Von Clausewitz

The unspoken word never does harm.

Lajos Kossuth

Anticipate the difficult by managing the easy.

Lao Tzu

Born to be wild - live to outgrow it.

Lao Tzu

Great acts are made up of small deeds.

Lao Tzu

He who talks more is sooner exhausted.

Lao Tzu

Knowing others is wisdom, knowing yourself is Enlightenment.

Lao Tzu

Mastering others is strength. Mastering yourself is true power.

Lao Tzu

Nature does not hurry, yet everything is accomplished.

Lao Tzu

Respond intelligently even to unintelligent treatment.

Lao Tzu

Silence is a source of great strength.

Lao Tzu

The journey of a thousand miles begins with one step.

Lao Tzu

To lead people walk behind them.

Lao Tzu

To see things in the seed, that is genius.

Lao Tzu

To the mind that is still, the whole universe surrenders.

Lao Tzu

For every ten jokes you acquire a hundred enemies.

Laurence Sterne

Men tire themselves in the pursuit of sleep.

Laurence Sterne

Pain and pleasure, like light and darkness, succeed each other.

Laurence Sterne

If you want to be happy, be.

Leo Tolstoy

The sole meaning of life is to serve humanity.

Leo Tolstoy

We lost because we told ourselves we lost.

Leo Tolstoy

Every generation is equidistant from God.

Leopold von Ranke

They are entitled to their freedom here.

Lewis Tappan

We will persevere, come life or death.

Lewis Tappan

Power corrupts, and absolute power corrupts absolutely.

Lord Acton

A proverb is the wisdom of many and the wit of one.

Lord Russell

I could sooner reconcile all Europe than two women.

Louis XIV

It is legal because I wish it.

Louis XIV

"Stay" is a charming word in a friend's vocabulary.

Louisa May Alcott

It takes two flints to make a fire.

Louisa May Alcott

Love is a great beautifier.

Louisa May Alcott

Clearness ornaments profound thoughts.

Luc de Clapiers

Great thoughts come from the heart.

Luc de Clapiers

Indolence is the sleep of the mind.

Luc de Clapiers

Obscurity is the realm of error.

Luc de Clapiers

One can not be just if one is not humane.

Luc de Clapiers

Patience is the art of hoping.

Luc de Clapiers

Prosperity makes few friends.

Luc de Clapiers

The conscience of the dying belies their life.

Luc de Clapiers

The Universe is worked and guided from within outwards.

Madame Blavatsky

Anticipate charity by preventing poverty.

Maimonides

You must accept the truth from whatever source it comes.

Maimonides

A man should be upright, not be kept upright.

Marcus Aurelius

A man's worth is no greater than his ambitions.

Marcus Aurelius

Anger cannot be dishonest.

Marcus Aurelius

Be content to seem what you really are.

Marcus Aurelius

Confine yourself to the present.

Marcus Aurelius

Each day provides its own gifts.

Marcus Aurelius

Men exist for the sake of one another.

Marcus Aurelius

Poverty is the mother of crime.

Marcus Aurelius

The art of living is more like wrestling than dancing.

Marcus Aurelius

Where a man can live, he can also live well.

Marcus Aurelius

Your life is what your thoughts make it.

Marcus Aurelius

How success changes the opinion of men!

Maria Edgeworth

Let them eat cake.

Marie Antoinette

There is nothing new except what has been forgotten.

Marie Antoinette

Even a stopped clock is right twice a day.

Marie von Ebner-Eschenbach

Imaginary evils are incurable.

Marie von Ebner-Eschenbach

In youth we learn; in age we understand.

Marie von Ebner-Eschenbach

Nobody knows enough, but many know too much.

Marie von Ebner-Eschenbach

Privilege is the greatest enemy of right.

Marie von Ebner-Eschenbach

What delights us in visible beauty is the invisible.

Marie von Ebner-Eschenbach

A man cannot be comfortable without his own approval.

Mark Twain

Action speaks louder than words but not nearly as often.

Mark Twain

Name the greatest of all inventors. Accident.

Mark Twain

Wrinkles should merely indicate where smiles have been.

Mark Twain

All universal moral principles are idle fancies.

Marquis de Sade

Truth titillates the imagination far less than fiction.

Marquis de Sade

Give the lady what she wants!

Marshall Field

Right or wrong, the customer is always right.

Marshall Field

Blood alone moves the wheels of history.

Martin Luther

Forgiveness is God's command.

Martin Luther

Nothing good ever comes of violence.

Martin Luther

Peace if possible, truth at all costs.

Martin Luther

Pray, and let God worry.

Martin Luther

Reason is a whore, the greatest enemy that faith has.

Martin Luther

The fewer the words, the better the prayer.

Martin Luther

When schools flourish, all flourishes.

Martin Luther

Pity is treason.

Maximilien Robespierre

The king must die so that the country can live.

Maximilien Robespierre

All God wants of man is a peaceful heart.

Meister Eckhart

Friends are the siblings God never gave us.

Mencius

Sincerity is the way to heaven.

Mencius

Truth uttered before its time is always dangerous.

Mencius

A wise man never loses anything, if he has himself.

Michel de Montaigne

Ambition is not a vice of little people.

Michel de Montaigne

An untempted woman cannot boast of her chastity.

Michel de Montaigne

Death, they say, acquits us of all obligations.

Michel de Montaigne

It is not death, it is dying that alarms me.

Michel de Montaigne

Lend yourself to others, but give yourself to yourself.

Michel de Montaigne

Marriage, a market which has nothing free but the entrance.

Michel de Montaigne

Not being able to govern events, I govern myself.

Michel de Montaigne

Poverty of goods is easily cured; poverty of soul, impossible.

Michel de Montaigne

The thing I fear most is fear.

Michel de Montaigne

The world is but a perpetual see-saw.

Michel de Montaigne

There are some defeats more triumphant than victories.

Michel de Montaigne

A closed mouth catches no flies.

Miguel de Cervantes

A person dishonored is worst than dead.

Miguel de Cervantes

A proverb is a short sentence based on long experience.

Miguel de Cervantes

Every man is the son of his own works.

Miguel de Cervantes

Fair and softly goes far.

Miguel de Cervantes

Fear has many eyes and can see things underground.

Miguel de Cervantes

Forewarned, forearmed; to be prepared is half the victory.

Miguel de Cervantes

God bears with the wicked, but not forever.

Miguel de Cervantes

He had a face like a blessing.

Miguel de Cervantes

He preaches well that lives well.

Miguel de Cervantes

Jests that give pains are no jests.

Miguel de Cervantes

Laziness never arrived at the attainment of a good wish.

Miguel de Cervantes

Man appoints, and God disappoints.

Miguel de Cervantes

No fathers or mothers think their own children ugly.

Miguel de Cervantes

Our hours in love have wings; in absence, crutches.

Miguel de Cervantes

That which costs little is less valued.

Miguel de Cervantes

The knowledge of yourself will preserve you from vanity.

Miguel de Cervantes

There's no taking trout with dry breeches.

Miguel de Cervantes

Those who'll play with cats must expect to be scratched.

Miguel de Cervantes

Thou hast seen nothing yet.

Miguel de Cervantes

To be prepared is half the victory.

Miguel de Cervantes

True valor lies between cowardice and rashness.

Miguel de Cervantes

Truth will rise above falsehood as oil above water.

Miguel de Cervantes

Virtue is the truest nobility.

Miguel de Cervantes

It is not strange... to mistake change for progress.

Millard Fillmore

Do nothing which is of no use.

Miyamoto Musashi

Perceive that which cannot be seen with the eye.

Miyamoto Musashi

I am, therefore there is a God.

Moses Mendelssohn

A celebrated people lose dignity upon a closer view.

Napolean Bonaparte

A Constitution should be short and obscure.

Napolean Bonaparte

A leader is a dealer in hope.

Napolean Bonaparte

A picture is worth a thousand words.

Napolean Bonaparte

A throne is only a bench covered with velvet.

Napolean Bonaparte

A true man hates no one.

Napolean Bonaparte

Ability is nothing without opportunity.

Napolean Bonaparte

An army marches on its stomach.

Napolean Bonaparte

Courage is like love; it must have hope for nourishment

Napolean Bonaparte

Forethought we may have, undoubtedly, but not foresight.

Napolean Bonaparte

Glory is fleeting, but obscurity is forever.

Napolean Bonaparte

He who fears being conquered is sure of defeat.

Napolean Bonaparte

History is a set of lies agreed upon.

Napolean Bonaparte

I have only one counsel for you - be master.

Napolean Bonaparte

I made all my generals out of mud.

Napolean Bonaparte

If you want a thing done well, do it yourself.

Napolean Bonaparte

Imagination rules the world.

Napolean Bonaparte

In politics stupidity is not a handicap.

Napolean Bonaparte

In politics... never retreat, never retract... never admit a mistake.

Napolean Bonaparte

It requires more courage to suffer than to die.

Napolean Bonaparte

Religion is excellent stuff for keeping common people quiet.

Napolean Bonaparte

Respect the burden.

Napolean Bonaparte

Soldiers generally win battles; generals get credit for them

Napolean Bonaparte

The army is the true nobility of our country.

Napolean Bonaparte

The best cure for the body is a quiet mind.

Napolean Bonaparte

The French complain of everything, and always.

Napolean Bonaparte

The infectiousness of crime is like that of the plague.

Napolean Bonaparte

The truest wisdom is a resolute determination.

Napolean Bonaparte

Victory belongs to the most persevering.

Napolean Bonaparte

War is the business of barbarians.

Napolean Bonaparte

We must laugh at man to avoid crying for him.

Napolean Bonaparte

Get there first with the most.

Nathan Bedford Forrest

Never stand and take a charge... charge them too.

Nathan Bedford Forrest

No damn man kills me and lives.

Nathan Bedford Forrest

A pure hand needs no glove to cover it.

Nathaniel Hawthorne

Easy reading is damn hard writing.

Nathaniel Hawthorne

Time flies over us, but leaves it shadow behind.

Nathaniel Hawthorne

A few honest men are better than numbers.

Oliver Cromwell

He who stops being better stops being good.

Oliver Cromwell

Necessity has no law.

Oliver Cromwell

Subtlety may deceive you; integrity never will.

Oliver Cromwell

We have met the enemy, and they are ours.

Oliver Perry

A journalist is a person who has mistaken their calling.

Otto von Bismarck

Politics is not an exact science.

Otto von Bismarck

Politics is the art of the next best.

Otto von Bismarck

Politics ruins the character.

Otto von Bismarck

When you want to fool the world, tell the truth.

Otto von Bismarck

Petty laws breed great crimes.

Ouida

Give me liberty or give me death.

Patrick Henry

If this be treason, make the most of it!

Patrick Henry

I can make men follow me to hell.

Philip Kearney

War is horrible because it strangles youth.

Philip Kearney

Either I will find a way, or I will make one.

Philip Sidney

The true science and study of man is man.

Pierre Charron

Communism is exploitation of the strong by the weak.

Pierre-Joseph Proudhon

When deeds speak, words are nothing.

Pierre-Joseph Proudhon

At the touch of love everyone becomes a poet.

Plato

Attention to health is life greatest hindrance.

Plato

Courage is a kind of salvation.

Plato

Courage is knowing what not to fear.

Plato

Cunning... is but the low mimic of wisdom.

Plato

Death is not the worst that can happen to men.

Plato

Democracy passes into despotism.

Plato

Friends have all things in common.

Plato

He was a wise man who invented beer.

Plato

Honesty is for the most part less profitable than dishonesty.

Plato

Ignorance, the root and the stem of every evil.

Plato

It is right to give every man his due.

Plato

Knowledge becomes evil if the aim be not virtuous.

Plato

Knowledge is true opinion.

Plato

Life must be lived as play.

Plato

Love is a serious mental disease.

Plato

Only the dead have seen the end of the war.

Plato

Opinion is the medium between knowledge and ignorance.

Plato

Philosophy begins in wonder.

Plato

Rhetoric is the art of ruling the minds of men.

Plato

The beginning is the most important part of the work.

Plato

The greatest wealth is to live content with little.

Plato

The wisest have the most authority.

Plato

There is no harm in repeating a good thing.

Plato

Thinking: the talking of the soul with itself.

Plato

We are twice armed if we fight with faith.

Plato

Wealth is well known to be a great comforter.

Plato

A few vices are sufficient to darken many virtues.

Plutarch

Whatever insults my State insults me.

Preston Brooks

There are two sides to every question.

Protagoras

Being pregnant is an occupational hazard of being a wife.

Queen Victoria

We excuse our sloth under the pretext of difficulty.

Quintilian

Avoid any specific discussion of public policy at public meetings.

Quintus Tullius Cicero

During war, the laws are silent.

Quintus Tullius Cicero

A friend is one before whom I may think aloud.

Ralph Waldo Emerson

A great man is always willing to be little.

Ralph Waldo Emerson

A man is what he thinks about all day long.

Ralph Waldo Emerson

Adopt the pace of nature: her secret is patience.

Ralph Waldo Emerson

All life is an experiment.

Ralph Waldo Emerson

An ounce of action is worth a ton of theory

Ralph Waldo Emerson

Every artist was first an amateur.

Ralph Waldo Emerson

Hitch your wagon to a star.

Ralph Waldo Emerson

It is not length of life, but depth of life.

Ralph Waldo Emerson

The only way to have a friend is to be one.

Ralph Waldo Emerson

We acquire the strength we have overcome.

Ralph Waldo Emerson

If you want to go east, don't go west.

Ramakrishna

When the flower blooms, the bees come uninvited.

Ramakrishna

Art includes everything that stimulates the desire to live.

Remy de Gourmont

Man has made use of his intelligence, he invented stupidity.

Remy de Gourmont

Simple ideas lie within the reach only of complex minds.

Remy de Gourmont

The woman who loves always smells good.

Remy de Gourmont

A minute's success pays the failure of years.

Robert Browning

And gain is gain, however small.

Robert Browning

Good, to forgive; best to forget.

Robert Browning

Ignorance is not innocence but sin.

Robert Browning

Love is energy of life.

Robert Browning

Motherhood: All love begins and ends there.

Robert Browning

Take away love and our earth is a tomb.

Robert Browning

The devil's name is dullness.

Robert E. Lee

Effective management always means asking the right question.

Robert Heller

Courage without conscience is a wild beast.

Robert Ingersoll

Hope is the only bee that makes honey without flowers.

Robert Ingersoll

Ignorance is the soil in which belief in miracles grows.

Robert Ingersoll

Kindness is the sunshine in which virtue grows.

Robert Ingersoll

No minister ever stood, or could stand, against public opinion.

Robert Peel

Better be killed than frightened to death.

Robert Smith Surtee

Freedom is always the freedom of dissenters.

Rosa Luxemburg

Those who do not move, do not notice their chains

Rosa Luxemburg

Hang 'em first, try 'em later.

Roy Bean

I know the law... I am it's greatest transgressor.

Roy Bean

A book is the only immortality.

Rufus Choate

Conscience is the authentic voice of God to you.

Rutherford B. Hayes

He serves his party best who serves his country best.

Rutherford B. Hayes

In some causes silence is dangerous.

Saint Ambrose

Give me chastity and continence, but not quite yet.

Saint Augustine

Hear the other side.

Saint Augustine

Punishment is justice for the unjust.

Saint Augustine

The purpose of all wars, is peace.

Saint Augustine

Teach us to give and not to count the cost.

Saint Ignatius

A fat stomach never breeds fine thoughts.

Saint Jerome

Never look a gift horse in the mouth.

Saint Jerome

The friendship that can cease has never been real.

Saint Jerome

The scars of others should teach us caution.

Saint Jerome

Be gentle to all and stern with yourself.

Saint Teresa of Avila

Pain is never permanent.

Saint Teresa of Avila

Every man is the architect of his own fortune.

Sallust

Necessity makes even the timid brave.

Sallust

We employ the mind to rule, the body to serve.

Sallust

Mankind are governed more by their feelings than by reason.

Samuel Adams

Handsome husbands often make a wife's heart ache.

Samuel Richardson

It is better to be thought perverse than insincere.

Samuel Richardson

Love before marriage is absolutely necessary.

Samuel Richardson

Love is not a volunteer thing.

Samuel Richardson

Nothing dries sooner than tears.

Samuel Richardson

Those we dislike can do nothing to please us.

Samuel Richardson

We are all very ready to believe what we like.

Samuel Richardson

Women do not often fall in love with philosophers.

Samuel Richardson

Every pint bottle should contain a quart.

Sir Boyle Roche

Half the lies our opponents tell about us are untrue.

Sir Boyle Roche

Beware the barrenness of a busy life.

Socrates

From the deepest desires often come the deadliest hate.

Socrates

It is not living that matters, but living rightly.

Socrates

The unexamined life is not worth living.

Socrates

Wisdom begins in wonder.

Socrates

It is the mind that makes the body.

Sojourner Truth

Truth is powerful and it prevails.

Sojourner Truth

Don't forget to love yourself.

Soren Kierkegaard

Love does not alter the beloved, it alters itself.

Soren Kierkegaard

Once you label me you negate me.

Soren Kierkegaard

One can advise comfortably from a safe port.

Soren Kierkegaard

Our life always expresses the result of our dominant thoughts.

Soren Kierkegaard

Man's heart away from nature becomes hard.

Standing Bear

Those who have happy homes seldom turn out badly.

Stonewall Jackson

All warfare is based on deception.

Sun Tzu

Opportunities multiply as they are seized.

Sun Tzu

Pretend inferiority and encourage his arrogance.

Sun Tzu

You have to believe in yourself.

Sun Tzu

Independence is happiness.

Susan B. Anthony

Suffrage is the pivotal right.

Susan B. Anthony

A bad peace is even worse than war.

Tacitus

Custom adapts itself to expediency.

Tacitus

Reason and judgment are the qualities of a leader

Tacitus

Things forbidden have a secret charm.

Tacitus

Show respect to all people, but grovel to none.

Tecumseh

Never violate the sacredness of your individual self-respect.

Theodore Parker

Outward judgment often fails, inward judgment never.

Theodore Parker

Politics is the science of urgencies.

Theodore Parker

Remorse is the pain of sin.

Theodore Parker

Wealth and want equally harden the human heart.

Theodore Parker

I am a part of everything that I have read.

Theodore Roosevelt

Nine-tenths of wisdom consists in being wise in time

Theodore Roosevelt

With self-discipline most anything is possible.

Theodore Roosevelt

Time is the most valuable thing a man can spend.

Theophrastus

The things that we love tell us what we are.

Thomas Aquinas

Well-ordered self-love is right and natural.

Thomas Aquinas

Nothing except the mint can make money without advertising.

Thomas B. Macaulay

The object of oratory alone in not truth, but persuasion.

Thomas B. Macaulay

Your Constitution is all sail and no anchor.

Thomas B. Macaulay

A loving heart is the beginning of all knowledge.

Thomas Carlyle

All great peoples are conservative.

Thomas Carlyle

Be not a slave of words.

Thomas Carlyle

Doubt, of whatever kind, can be ended by action alone.

Thomas Carlyle

Every noble work is at first impossible.

Thomas Carlyle

Necessity dispenseth with decorum.

Thomas Carlyle

No person is important enough to make me angry.

Thomas Carlyle

No pressure, no diamonds.

Thomas Carlyle

No violent extreme endures.

Thomas Carlyle

Silence is more eloquent than words.

Thomas Carlyle

The world is a republic of mediocrities, and always was.

Thomas Carlyle

Thought is the parent of the deed.

Thomas Carlyle

Weak eyes are fondest of glittering objects.

Thomas Carlyle

Work alone is noble.

Thomas Carlyle

A good garden may have some weeds.

Thomas Fuller

A man is not good or bad for one action.

Thomas Fuller

A wise man turns chance into good fortune.

Thomas Fuller

Bad excuses are worse than none

Thomas Fuller

Better be alone than in bad company.

Thomas Fuller

Every horse thinks its own pack heaviest.

Thomas Fuller

Great hopes make great men.

Thomas Fuller

Nothing is easy to the unwilling.

Thomas Fuller

One that would have the fruit must climb the tree.

Thomas Fuller

The fool wanders, a wise man travels.

Thomas Fuller

Force and fraud are in war the two cardinal virtues.

Thomas Hobbes

It is not wisdom but Authority that makes a law.

Thomas Hobbes

Leisure is the Mother of Philosophy.

Thomas Hobbes

It's more than a game. It's an institution.

Thomas Hughes

Always mystify, mislead and surprise the enemy if possible.

Thomas J. Jackson

Always take hold of things by the smooth handle

Thomas Jefferson

An enemy generally says and believes what he wishes.

Thomas Jefferson

An injured friend is the bitterest of foes.

Thomas Jefferson

Be polite to all, but intimate with few.

Thomas Jefferson

Delay is preferable to error.

Thomas Jefferson

Every generation needs a new revolution.

Thomas Jefferson

He who knows best knows how little he knows.

Thomas Jefferson

Honesty is the first chapter in the book of wisdom.

Thomas Jefferson

Information is the currency of democracy.

Thomas Jefferson

Money, not morality, is the principle commerce of civilized nations.

Thomas Jefferson

Never put off till tomorrow what you can do today.

Thomas Jefferson

Never spend your money before you have earned it.

Thomas Jefferson

Power is not alluring to pure minds.

Thomas Jefferson

The boisterous sea of liberty is never without a wave.

Thomas Jefferson

The most successful war seldom pays for its losses.

Thomas Jefferson

We did not raise armies for glory or for conquest.

Thomas Jefferson

We never repent of having eaten too little.

Thomas Jefferson

History is Philosophy teaching by examples.

Thucydides

Ignorance is bold and knowledge reserved.

Thucydides

The secret of freedom, courage.

Thucydides

It becomes an emperor to die standing.

Titus

The body of a dead enemy always smells sweet.

Titus

Between two evils, choose neither; between two goods, choose both.

Tyron Edwards

Labor disgraces no man, but occasionally men disgrace labor.

Ulysses S. Grant

Let us have peace.

Ulysses S. Grant

My failures have been errors in judgment, not of intent.

Ulysses S. Grant

Nations, like individuals, are punished for their transgressions.

Ulysses S. Grant

The church and state forever separate.

Ulysses S. Grant

Ignorance is the primary source of all misery and vice.

Victor Cousin

A man should never neglect his family for business.

Walt Disney

If you can dream it, you can do it.

Walt Disney

It's kind of fun to do the impossible.

Walt Disney

Laughter is America's most important export.

Walt Disney

Truth is inner harmony.

Walter Rathenau

For success, attitude is equally as important as ability.

Walter Scott

Look back, and smile on perils past.

Walter Scott

Success - keeping your mind awake and your desire asleep.

Walter Scott

Age is a matter of feeling, not of years.

Washington Irving

Great minds have purposes; others have wishes.

Washington Irving

There is never jealousy where there is not strong regard

Washington Irving

Agitation is the atmosphere of the brains

Wendell Phillips

Aristocracy is always cruel.

Wendell Phillips

Christianity is a battle not a dream.

Wendell Phillips

Difference of religion breeds more quarrels than difference of politics.

Wendell Phillips

Many know how to flatter, few know how to praise.

Wendell Phillips

Responsibility educates.

Wendell Phillips

The heart is the best reflective thinker.

Wendell Phillips

The keener the want the lustier the growth.

Wendell Phillips

Peace rules the day, where reason rules the mind.

Wilkie Collins

Better a bad excuse, than none at all.

William Camden

The early bird catches the worm.

William Camden

The sea hath fish for every man.

William Camden

To be poor and independent is very nearly an impossibility

William Cobbett

You never know what you can do till you try.

William Cobbett

The dread of criticism is the death of genius.

William Gilmore Simms

The only true source of politeness is consideration.

William Gilmore Simms

Justice delayed is justice denied.

William Gladstone

Nothing that is morally wrong can be politically right.

William Gladstone

The very air in which you live is an inspiration.

William Henry Moody

The public be damned.

William Henry Vanderbilt

Begin to be now what you will be hereafter.

William James

Belief creates the actual fact.

William James

In business for yourself, not by yourself.

William James

Is life worth living? It all depends on the liver.

William James

Man can alter his life by altering his thinking.

William James

Pessimism leads to weakness, optimism to power.

William James

To change ones life: Start immediately. Do it flamboyantly.

William James

A good laugh is sunshine in the house.

William Makepeace Thackeray

Bravery never goes out of fashion.

William Makepeace Thackeray

Dinner was made for eating, not for talking.

William Makepeace Thackeray

Follow your honest convictions and be strong.

William Makepeace Thackeray

I would rather make my name than inherit it.

William Makepeace Thackeray

Next to excellence is the appreciation of it.

William Makepeace Thackeray

People hate as they love, unreasonably.

William Makepeace Thackeray

Expositions are the timekeepers of progress.

William McKinley

In the time of darkest defeat, victory may be nearest.

William McKinley

Our differences are politics. Our agreements are principles.

William McKinley

Force may make hypocrites, but it can never make converts.

William Penn

He that lives to forever, never fears dying.

William Penn

Knowledge is the treasure of a wise man.

William Penn

Only trust thyself, and another shall not betray thee.

William Penn

Rarely promise, but, if lawful, constantly perform.

William Penn

Rebellion to tyrants is obedience to God.

William Penn

Confidence is a plant of slow growth in an aged heart.

William Pitt

Unlimited power corrupts the possessor.

William Pitt

Whatever enlarges hope will also exalt courage.

William Samuel Johnson

Whatever you have, spend less.

William Samuel Johnson

Be great in act, as you have been in thought.

William Shakespeare

Better a witty fool than a foolish wit.

William Shakespeare

Better three hours too soon than a minute too late.

William Shakespeare

Expectation is the root of all heartache.

William Shakespeare

Ill deeds are doubled with an evil word.

William Shakespeare

In time we hate that which we often fear.

William Shakespeare

Love all, trust a few, do wrong to none.

William Shakespeare

Love looks not with the eyes, but with the mind.

William Shakespeare

No legacy is so rich as honesty.

William Shakespeare

Strong reasons make strong actions.

William Shakespeare

This above all: to thine own self be true.

William Shakespeare

War is hell.

William Tecumseh Sherman

War is too serious a matter to leave to soldiers.

William Tecumseh Sherman

You cannot qualify war in harsher terms than I will.

William Tecumseh Sherman

We come to beginnings only at the end.

William Throsby Bridges

Every man dies. Not every man really lives.

William Wallace

People don't follow titles, they follow courage.

William Wells Brown

Every failure is a step to success.

William Whewell

It takes a wise man to recognize a wise man.

Xenophanes

Fast is fine, but accuracy is everything.

Xenophon

The sweetest of all sounds is praise.

Xenophon

Pride and excess bring disaster for man.

Xun Zi

Happiness is the absence of the striving for happiness.

Zhuangzi

Rewards and punishments are the lowest form of education.

Zhuangzi

Those who realize their folly are not true fools.

Zhuangzi

www.ingramcontent.com/pod-product-compliance
Lightning Source LLC
Chambersburg PA
CBHW081356280526
45788CB00009B/2904